HANDLE LEGAL ISSUES LIKE A PRO

HANDLE LEGAL ISSUES LIKE A PRO

50+ TIPS

FORECLOSURE | REAL ESTATE | COLLECTIONS

Sade Ogunbode, J.D.

Disclaimer

Nothing in this publication should be construed as specific legal advice for your particular situation. For case-specific legal advice, please contact our office directly. Please note also that most of the content of this book is geared towards Texas state law.

The author has strived to be as accurate and complete as possible in the creation of this book. In practical advice books, like anything else in life, there are no guarantees.

Readers are cautioned to apply their own judgment about their individual circumstances and act accordingly. Readers are advised to seek services of competent professionals in the legal, business, and finance fields as needed.

First Edition: August 2016
ISBN: 1533595704
ISBN-13: 978-1533595706

To law firm Staff, Clients, Friends, Mentors, and Colleagues:
Your endless support is forever appreciated.

About

This publication is brought to you by the lawyer author, as a summary reference guide to highlight the most common questions and scenarios regularly encountered at her law firm. This is by no means an exhaustive or detailed guide, but rather, an abbreviated version of the facts of the cases routinely handled at the firm. The scenarios described are for illustration purposes only. In practice, the facts of each case will naturally vary more or less and unique solutions will need to be designed for each situation.

The author is the founder and principal of a Texas based Practice providing legal counseling, coaching, and representation with a focus on Real Estate, Consumer Rights, and Civil Litigation. The litigation practice includes Collections Defense, Foreclosure Defense, and Contract Disputes.

Should you see yourself, a friend, or loved one in any of the situations or stories below, in need of legal guidance, or have a similar fact pattern to any of the scenarios listed below, you may contact the law firm directly. The law firm's information is provided below. A burden shared is a burden halved.

Law Office of Sade Ogunbode
7703 N. Lamar Blvd. Ste. 400
Austin, TX 78752
P: 512.693.7117
www.everymanlaw.com
admin@everymanlaw.com

Author Bio:

Sade is an avid traveler, music lover, foodie, and a self-improvement and empowerment enthusiast.

She is licensed to practice law in the state of Texas and is admitted to the United States Bankruptcy Court. She holds a Texas Mediator license and approaches the practice of law with an attitude of excellence, fairness, and compassion.

She enjoys volunteer work involving children and women, helping on advisory boards, and giving educational presentations to the public on relevant legal issues.

Free Legal Tips, Blog Posts & Video Help:

The author provides free legal tips to friends, clients and potential clients, through the law firm website and Facebook page. These free resources may be accessed by visiting the law firm website on www.everymanlaw.com.

Contents

FREQUENTLY ASKED QUESTIONS

COLLECTIONS | REPOSSESSION | CREDIT

My law firm receives lots of questions regarding old debts, judgments and credit reports. In this section, I have covered the most frequently asked questions in regards to collections, vehicle loans and credit report issues. In the next few pages, you'll find general tips on the first steps to take in order to be proactive about any matter. That way, you can set yourself up for a positive outcome, and set your case up for success, even if you end up hiring a lawyer to help you.

I've been sued by a creditor. I know I owe the money so I don't have any defenses, right?

It depends. Most debtor defendants have at least one or two defenses. It could be that the amount requested is incorrect or unreasonably high, or even that you weren't correctly served with notice of the lawsuit. There are many different types of defenses to collection suits. At the very least, you should do the following:

1. **Respond Promptly** - Whatever you do, you should at least respond to the lawsuit. Answers to lawsuits are time-sensitive so you must act quickly. There is a specific process when arguing that you were incorrectly served and this must be pled in your very first response. You may need an attorney's guidance on this one so that you don't unknowingly waive any defense.
2. **Avoid Default Judgment** - You want to avoid the other party sneaking to court and getting a money judgment against you. So, keep on top of the case. A judgment creditor can later try to freeze your bank account, seize assets etc. A judgment may also go on your credit report as a public record and negatively affect your credit score and ability to get new credit.
3. **General Denial** - You can at the very least, make a general denial defense when you don't know if all the information in the complaint is true or if you think the information in the complaint is not right. You may later amend your answer to add more defenses. NOTE that some defenses such as statute of limitations must be argued upfront in your initial response.

I've been sued for non-payment on a credit account. Is there any hope?

Yes. You almost always have a defense to a collection suit. A procedural, statutory or other defense could result in a dismissal, or provide the leverage needed to obtain a reasonable settlement.

The other party (the plaintiff) has the burden to prove that you owe the debt in the amount sued for, and that the plaintiff is the rightful party to be collecting on the debt. Most times the plaintiff will not follow the correct procedure to bring the lawsuit, or will not meet the burden of proof required for the plaintiff to prevail.

A collections' defense attorney can usually quickly spot the defenses that an untrained eye cannot, and use them as leverage. At the very least, the attorney will help you negotiate the debt down to something very manageable, and can negotiate for the settlement to be paid in installments over several months if needed.

Settlements normally vary from between 40% to 80% of the total sued for, but the lawyer may be able to negotiate a lower settlement depending on the facts of each particular case.

How can I avoid getting a judgment against me?

You can be proactive by participating in the lawsuit (if one has already been filed), or settling with the other party. Participate in the lawsuit by answering to the complaint, and showing up for all hearings. Even so, you may still end up with a judgment if no settlement can be reached and the court rules against you. Whenever in doubt, consult a lawyer to help you minimize the chances of getting a judgment against you.

What's so bad about having a judgment against me?

It will affect your credit score and overall credit worthiness. The credit score affects all aspects of life such as interest rates, credit limit, renting, insurance quotes, employment etc.

Most importantly, the judgment will hang over your head for 10 years and may even be renewed every 10 years. This means the judgment creditor can surprise you at any time by freezing your bank account, seizing your assets etc. Additionally, you won't qualify for a mortgage loan with a judgment on your credit report.

If I can't pay what I owe, do I have to declare bankruptcy?

Not necessarily. You should first explore debt consolidation, a lengthy payment plan, a discounted settlement, or a combination of all these arrangements. As a last resort, you may consider bankruptcy. Our law firm usually advises people to use bankruptcy only as a last resort because it too will affect your credit score and credit worthiness significantly.

Can I pay a small amount over time to settle my debt?

Yes, you can, if the creditor agrees to that type of arrangement. Most creditors will agree to such arrangement.

Can I buy time to save up the money to pay off a debt or judgment?

Yes, you will have to work something out with the creditor where your payments do not start for a few months. Our firm often helps clients delay the start of the repayment period. If unable to work it out on your own, a lawyer should be able to help.

I heard that the Statute of Limitations in collection cases is 4 years. Does that mean the creditor cannot collect if I haven't paid on the debt for 4 years?

Yes, generally speaking, but statute of limitations is not always straightforward to calculate. That defense can be tricky. A lot of factors go into determining when the clock starts. Sometimes, the clock is restarted all over again due to certain actions on the part of the parties.

Can a creditor come by to confront me at work?

Under federal law, a debt collector cannot communicate with you at work once he/she knows that your employer prohibits such communication. However, this law does not apply to the creditor. A creditor can come by your job but still doesn't have the right to harass or publicly embarrass you. The creditor is the party that you owe the debt to, the debt collector is an agent working for the creditor.

Can creditors garnish my wages in Texas?

Generally, creditors cannot garnish wages but can reach those wages once already in your bank account, by levying (freezing) the account. Wages cannot be garnished by most creditors, EXCEPT in the following situations:

1. For child support.
2. For spousal maintenance (alimony).
3. For federal student loans that are in default.
4. For unpaid income taxes.

Myth: If child support is coming out of a paycheck, the wages cannot be garnished for anything else.

Fact: Wages can be garnished for other types of obligations even if already being garnished for child support. However, there are percentage limits on how much may be garnished.

How can I resolve a judgment on my credit report if I can't locate the creditor?

If there is a judgment on your credit report, you can still settle it by making an offer to the judgment creditor. Try your best to locate the judgment creditor using Google searches, online people or entity finder tools etc.

If unable to locate the creditor, you will have to pay the full amount of the judgment into the court registry (account). The court will hold the money until the judgment creditor resurfaces to claim it.

Once you've paid the debt into the court registry, the court will approve a Release of Judgment which will clear up the public record and you will also use the Release to clear up your credit report.

When can a judgment be removed from credit reports?

Following a judgment from the court, the judgment creditor (plaintiff) usually orders an Abstract of Judgment from the court clerk. An abstract of judgment is a summary of the judgment. The abstract is then filed in the county's real property records and picked up by credit bureaus. This is usually how the judgment ends up showing on a credit report.

Judgments are normally good for 10 years i.e. will show up on the credit report for 10 years. After 10 years, the judgment then becomes dormant unless renewed. If the judgment is dormant, you can get it off of your credit report at this point.

You should try settling the debt if you need to improve your credit or are in the process of purchasing a home. Settling will normally only show the item as "Settled", "Satisfied" or "Paid in Full" and won't get you a complete removal of the item.

However, it is sufficient for most mortgage lenders and creditors. A good lawyer will be able to negotiate complete removal of the judgment at any time, by getting the judgment vacated.

My vehicle was stolen. Do I still owe the loan balance?

Yes. The theft does not undo the contract between you and the finance company. Full coverage auto insurance is the safety net that you have in this type of situation. Continue to make your car payments until you file an insurance claim. Insurance policies do not usually cover overdue car payments.

Depending on your policy, the insurer will sometimes pay off the full loan balance, less any deductible. Otherwise, the insurer will pay market value to the finance company - up to the policy limits. If there is a balance owed after the insurance payment is applied to the loan balance, you will still be liable for that remaining balance.

I voluntarily surrendered my vehicle. Can the finance company still come after me or my co-signer?

Possibly. Your co-signer assumes the same responsibility as you. In simple terms, if you owe any money to the creditor, your co-signer also owes the money to the creditor. The same goes for all contracts where you have a co-signer.

After a repossession (voluntary or involuntary), the vehicle is sold and the money received is applied to the debt/ loan balance. If there is still a balance remaining (deficiency) you still owe the creditor. Also, some creditors will charge you for tuning up/ cleaning up the vehicle in preparation for the sale, and also for storing the vehicle on their lot.

Most times, you or a lawyer can negotiate down the amount of such deficiency. A lawyer may be in a better position to negotiate to where the voluntary repossession does not reflect negatively on your credit report.

FREQUENTLY ASKED QUESTIONS

MORTGAGE | FORECLOSURE | EVICTION

The lending industry came under increased scrutiny in recent years and some government agencies sued several lenders. Private causes of action are available also but the path is full of obstacles. Justice shouldn't be about who has the deepest pockets or can hire the biggest firms, but sadly, it often is.

Lenders have been found to engage in deficient training, underwriting and disclosure, all while relying on the convenience of the so called "bailouts" (government insurance on the mortgage loans). This book will not cover these issues in detail but I'll provide some helpful tips for dealing with real estate lenders.

This section contains common questions regarding mortgages, foreclosure, eviction and other real estate related matters. I'm of the belief that timely knowledge is power.

I recently received foreclosure letters from my lender. What are my options?

The best first step is to get a complete mortgage evaluation and status report - this can be done by an attorney who works in the field of foreclosure defense. This is essentially a thorough mortgage audit of the loan transaction and review of the chain of title, in an attempt to spot any issues with chain of title, or issues raised by securitization of the loan.

The goal is to put you in a position where you can settle the case with the lender without need for litigation. However, keep in mind that it isn't always possible to avoid litigation. Whatever you do, do not try to handle this by yourself as it is doubly difficult to reverse the sale once the foreclosure sale has happened.

I was served a 736 foreclosure lawsuit. What can I do?

A 736 lawsuit is a request for an order permitting foreclosure. You should file a response within the allotted time. This is currently 38 days in the state of Texas. Discovery and counterclaims are not permitted in a 736 proceeding. However, you may file a separate lawsuit where you sue the lender and state your own claims. A separate lawsuit to quiet title will automatically put a stop to the foreclosure lawsuit.

Can I still reinstate my loan even if the foreclosure date has been set or ordered?

Yes. Most times you can reinstate up until the time of the foreclosure, or even following the foreclosure. Texas does not have a legal right to redemption except for tax-lien foreclosures and HOA foreclosures. However, a lot of deeds (contract with the lender) have a reinstatement clause that gives you the right to reinstate even when foreclosure is pending. Additionally, even if you are outside the timeframe provided in your deed, some lenders will still allow reinstatement as long as you tender the full amount that is back-owed.

Am I entitled to loan modification on my mortgage?

No. A loan modification is essentially an agreement to modify the original terms of the loan, hence, optional.

Under the Home Affordable Modification Program (HAMP) guidelines, you are *only entitled to being considered* for a loan modification. You are entitled to be considered, if you meet the minimum eligibility requirements. Most homeowners are eligible. Still, the lender is only required to consider your application in good faith etc. My experience is that most of the lenders out there simply go through the motions with no intention of actually granting a modification.

So, if you happen to be one of the few that actually get approved for a loan modification, don't miss any payments, pay late, or break the modification agreement in any way. It may be the only chance you get to keep your home. That being said, your attorney can usually get things moving faster when trying to get a loan modification. Good luck!

If I do a short sale will I still owe anything to the lender?

Possibly. Short sale means the sale proceeds will not cover all liens (mortgage, HOA lien etc.). Lenders will sometimes agree to a short sale when a borrower wishes to avoid foreclosure. Most borrowers mistakenly assume that the lender has also agreed to write off any deficiency. However, this isn't always the case. To avoid any unpleasant surprises, it is best to negotiate a waiver of deficiency and obtain a written agreement indicating that the deficiency will be waived.

Can my mortgage company force me to do a short sale?

No. The mortgage company cannot force a short sale. You have the right to explore all foreclosure prevention options. Some of the better options are listed below. Enlist the help of an attorney if needed and see if you qualify for:

1. Reinstatement – pay back-owed amount in full.
2. Repayment plan – make small payments until paid.
3. Forbearance agreement – defer to back-end of loan.
4. Loan modification – change the contract terms.

Can I get my home back if it is already foreclosed?

Yes, sometimes. It's easier if the property was auctioned using a credit bid i.e. the lender bought it back. If a third party won the auction, it is more challenging but still possible depending on the facts of your case. You will need to move fast and ask for a rescission and reversal of the sale.

You most likely will be required to show proof of funds for reinstatement of your mortgage. The proof must be in the form of certified funds such as cashier's check or money order and must reflect enough funds to cover any arrears plus any current mortgage due.

What if I never received a notice of foreclosure? Is the foreclosure still valid?

If the lender can prove that the notice was mailed to you at your property address, then, that is all that is required by law. Whether you actually get the notice is not within the lender's control. The law only requires that lenders properly mail the notice. Lenders usually send the notices via certified mail plus regular mail. The best way to prevent a nasty surprise is to open all mail and claim all mail that is sent to your address.

What if my mortgage payment was lost in the mail?

Since the lender is not responsible for the loss of your payment, you will have to address the issue with your mail carrier. Left unpaid, you will be in default under the terms of your agreement. The lender may then start collection efforts and you'll have to cure the default (pay back-owed amount).

What if foreclosure proceeds are more than debt owed?

Sometimes, the foreclosure sale price is higher than the debt owed on a foreclosed mortgage. Texas law states that the original homeowner who owed under the mortgage / promissory note, has the right to the excess funds. However, lenders and their agents aren't in a rush to release these funds. Sometimes, the excess is applied to the lender's collection costs. In such a situation, the homeowner may end up recovering little to no portion of the excess funds.

Related Question: How do I know if my home sold for more than what I owed at the time of the foreclosure? If you suspect that this may be the case, it's best to get a lawyer or a real estate agent to look into the matter for you. A lawyer can request an accounting and verify that you get what you're entitled to under the law. An accounting is an itemized detail of the proceeds of sale, as well as any costs that have been deducted from those proceeds.

Can the mortgage lender foreclose against a deceased borrower?

No. Lenders may not properly foreclose against a deceased borrower. Under Texas law, title to the secured property immediately vests in the heirs-at-law at the moment of death. Therefore, the heirs will have ownership interest in the property and the lender must send notice to those heirs before foreclosing.

Lenders may proceed with the foreclose as long as proper steps are taken e.g. notice to heirs etc. If foreclosure takes place against a deceased person without proper notice to the heirs, the heirs have the right to contest the foreclosure.

If the lender forecloses against a deceased person, that lender has inadvertently extinguished the note and security instrument which are the things holding the contract together in the first place. The foreclosure will then be voidable but not necessarily void.

I received a 3-Day Notice to Vacate. Do I have to move out by the end of the 3 days?

No. The person who issued the notice has to wait the full 3 days. If you don't move out, the other party will have to sue you to get the court's permission to evict you. The deadlines are very short so, open all mail and make sure to file an answer if you intend to fight the eviction. There is usually a hearing date listed in the court documents that are served. Most times you have less than a week to respond and prepare for the eviction hearing. You should promptly file an answer and be sure to appear in court to defend yourself as needed.

I was told that I have 5 days to appeal an eviction judgment, does a holiday or weekend count?

Weekends and holidays count, unless the last day falls on a weekend or holiday. The day of the eviction judgment doesn't count. For example, if you received a judgment today, Day 1 is tomorrow. You will count five days then stop. If Day 5 is a Saturday, Sunday or court observed holiday, you have until the next working day to file your appeal.

Can I use a Quit Claim Deed to buy or transfer property?

Yes, but we strongly advise against it because a Quit Claim Deed does not *guarantee* good title to property. The Quit Claim Deed simply states that whatever interest the party conveying has in the property, he/she conveys to the second party. The first party does not guarantee to defend against any future claimants that show up to challenge the ownership of the second party.

Also, when the current property owner is ready to sell, most title companies in Texas will not issue a title policy to insure title unless the original seller signs a warranty deed to convey the property. Alternatively, the title companies will want to see a court order that unequivocally indicates the type of ownership interest that the current owner has in the property.

If the original seller cannot be located, or refuses to sign a warranty deed for whatever reason, the current owner will have to file suit to quiet title. This makes things more complicated and results in delays and additional costs.

What exactly is a Quiet Title case?

A Quiet Title action is an equitable remedy for removing a cloud on title to real estate. A cloud on title is caused by an encumbrance, hindrance, or claim to title by another party.

The Quiet Title lawsuit is filed in order to obtain a court order from the court declaring an opposing party's (defendant) claims invalid or ineffective and confirming that the person who filed (plaintiff) is the rightful owner of the property. The plaintiff proves his/her right to title by showing that a particular defendant (or any other claimant) has a weaker claim to title than the plaintiff does.

What is Trespass-to-Try-Title?

Trespass-to-Try-Title is similar to a Quiet Title action but is a legal remedy i.e. it's provided for by statute. The evidence needed to prove the case is therefore different. Trespass to real estate occurs when a person "enters" (encroaches) another's land without consent.

This commonly occurs in the context of boundary line disputes. For example, a neighbor's fence may be placed such that it wrongfully takes over some of your land. If the neighbor refuses to move the fence, then a Trespass-to-Try-Title lawsuit may be necessary.

Is it illegal for a mortgage company to give me a Home Equity loan if I have an agricultural use exemption on my property?

Yes, with a couple of exceptions. As a general rule, the law prohibits lenders from giving home equity loans out on properties that have AG-Use exemption. There is an exception made for situations where the AG-Use exemption is solely for milk production. In that case, the home equity loan is not illegal.

The second exception is that if the residence can be carved out such that the portion covered by the home equity loan is not covered by the AG-Use exemption, then the loan is not illegal.

FREQUENTLY ASKED QUESTIONS

CIVIL LITIGATION

In this section, I have covered select questions that many clients have regarding litigation (lawsuits). Litigation is full of procedural traps and can be tricky unless one is well-versed in the procedural rules for each particular case and each court. For this reason, I strongly advise you to consult with an attorney if a matter is already in the litigation phase. Due to the complexity of the litigation process, I am only able to cover some less technical questions in the following pages. I hope that you find the material useful.

Can a judge force me to go to mediation?

Yes. A lot of courts now mandate mediation in certain cases. You are required to at least try mediation first to see if issues can be resolved outside the courtroom.

Once you get to the mediation table, you are not required to settle against your own best interests. No mediator, judge or attorney can force you to settle. If you need more time to prepare for the mediation, you can request more time, or if you have good reason to object to mediation, you may file an objection (usually within 10 days from the time you get the notice of mediation).

I didn't know I was being recorded! Will the judge allow the recording to be used as evidence?

Yes, unless the other side fails to lay the proper foundation. Unlike most states, Texas allows for "one party consent" when it comes to recording conversations. As long as one person consents to the recording, it is lawful. Don't sweat it too much if this happens. Most recordings aren't as good (incriminating) as the recording party thinks. Naturally, the other person will be on his/her best behavior when secretly recording you. The judge is well aware of this type of bias and your attorney will also remind the judge so that you are not unfairly disadvantaged.

What exactly is discovery?

Discovery is a mechanism by which a litigant (party to a lawsuit) is able to obtain information from another party in the lawsuit, or from a third party related to the lawsuit. It is specifically provided for under the law and comes in different forms. Common forms of discovery include Requests for Disclosure, Requests for Admissions, Requests for

Production, Deposition, Subpoena of Records, and Written Interrogatories.

Once discovery is served on a party, by law, that party has a specific number of days to respond. Some objections are permitted as well as claims of privilege i.e. that the information requested is privileged under the attorney-client or other privilege. Parties can agree to extensions of the answer period, and there can sometimes be several rounds of discovery before a case is finalized.

Do I have to respond to the opposing party's Requests for Production of Documents?

Yes, you have to respond. Both plaintiff and defendant (or petitioner and respondent) have a right to serve discovery on the other party to get some information that will help decide the issues in the case. There are different forms of discovery and different forms of responses. For example, you may provide a requested document or object to the request. Discovery is governed by the local rules of civil procedure and the rules are very technical. The results of any misstep may be dire and ignorance of the law is never an acceptable excuse in court. Due to the high stakes, it's best to have an attorney assist you in answering any discovery.

I received a Notice of Judgment - I missed the hearing date for trial. Is it too late now to do anything?

If just now receiving a notice of judgment, it is probably not too late. In Texas state courts, you have 30 days from the date of the final judgment to challenge the judgment. The time is shorter for your first appeal in an eviction case. Since you were not present at the trial, the opposing party would have gotten what we call a "default judgment". You can try challenging a default judgment by asking for the default judgment to be set aside and requesting a new trial. Federal courts have different but similar rules.

If you did not get the Notice of Judgment at all, but found out about the judgment (e.g. saw it on a credit report), or if you received the notice after the 30 days already passed, there are still ways to challenge the default judgment. The sooner you act, the better because there are lots of other deadlines to consider such as the deadline to file an appeal if needed. A timely filed challenge to a default judgment will extend the time to file an appeal. It's best to seek a lawyer's help.

I received a Waiver of Citation and Service. Should I sign the Waiver?

Waivers can come in many forms. A waiver of citation or service is one that allows a petitioner (person who filed a petition with the court) to carry on with a legal matter that affects your rights, without formally serving you with papers. That is, the petitioner does not have to hire a process server to serve you with those court papers or otherwise formally serve you via mail or other mandated methods of service.

If you receive a waiver letter from an attorney, it should be accompanied with a petition or some other legal document that was filed with the court. The letter should tell you exactly what rights you are waiving. Most often, you are waiving your right to formal service but may also be waiving your right to notice of future proceedings in the case such as hearings. Before you sign the waiver, read the petition and make sure you fully understand the right(s) that you are waiving.

Whenever in doubt, consult an attorney to make sure you are not waiving rights that will come back to hurt you. Remember, the other party's attorney doesn't work for you. So, be sure to do your due diligence and protect your rights.

What is a Notice of Intention to Take Oral Deposition?

The Notice of Intention to Take Oral Deposition is commonly used in conjunction with the Subpoena Duces Tecum. Depositions are one form of discovery in legal cases. Discovery is how parties get information and evidence from each other. The Notice means that the opposing side will like to ask you questions in person, under oath, and record your responses. Depositions usually take place in the lawyer's office or the office of a court reporter.

The Subpoena Duces Tecum means that you are to appear at the specified location with certain documents that are listed. Some objections exist that you can use if you don't want to appear for the deposition or produce documents. Your lawyer will be able to determine what objections are applicable to your case. You may also file a Motion for Protection or to Quash or Limit the subpoena.

Otherwise, you must appear and produce the documents as requested. Failure to appear is considered a discovery violation. The other party can then file a Motion to Compel and ask the court for monetary sanctions/fines against you.

There has been no activity on my case for months. Will the court dismiss my case?

Possibly. Different courts have different internal procedures for handling dormant cases. Some courts will keep a dormant case on their dockets for years. Most courts will dismiss the case after two years of inactivity. However, the parties and their counsel will receive a notice warning them that the case is about to be dismissed. Any of the parties can they ask for the court to retain the case on the docket so that it is not dismissed. The court may require a hearing unless all parties are in agreement to retain the case on the docket.

I sued someone and the trial is in a few days but we just worked something out. What do I need to do?

If settlement is reached outside of Court, you can call the clerk and do one of the following things, or you can wait till the hearing date and request the same thing once in front of the judge. Request for the court or judge to:

Suspend the Lawsuit (Postpone Trial Date)

You, as the plaintiff, may suspend the lawsuit until you have the money in your hands or any other thing agreed upon. Ask the judge for a "continuance". The judge may ask how long you want - could be 7 days, 10 days, or 3 months etc. You want to suspend the hearing if you are not a hundred percent sure that the defendant will honor the new agreement. This way, if the defendant fails to deliver on his/her promise, you can easily resume the case and ask for a new trial date.

Dismiss the Lawsuit

This is best if the defendant has paid you what's owed, prior to the trial date. You can ask the court to dismiss the lawsuit entirely.

What does it mean when the court strikes a pleading?

It means that the court has agreed to make a filed document (pleading) ineffective and removed the pleading from the case record almost as if it were never filed.

What does it mean to quash service of citation?

It means the court has agreed that the service of the court document on a party was not properly done. The improper service is quashed as if the recipient was never served at all.

BRIEF CASE STUDIES

REAL SOLUTIONS FOR REAL LIFE SCENARIOS

At our law firm, we pride ourselves on holding companies, especially mortgage lenders, accountable to consumers. However, there are other situations that arise outside of the context of consumer rights' violations. In this section, I cover a variety of issues relating to real estate and credit transactions, not only issues relating to mortgage lenders.

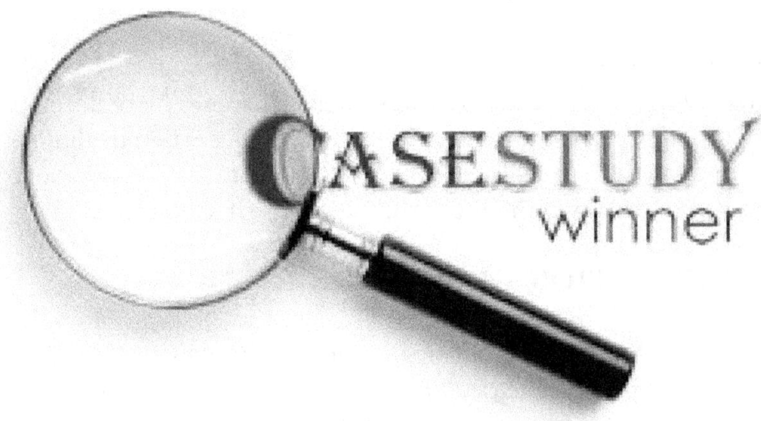

1. AFFIDAVIT OF HEIRSHIP

Bob and Sue are brother and sister born to the same mother and father. Bob and Sue also have two half-brothers from their father's previous marriage. Their father recently passed away. He wasn't married at the time of his death and owned only a McMansion and several life insurance policies. No will was found but he named Bob and Sue as beneficiaries on his life insurance policies. All four children agree that they are all entitled to dad's McMansion and agree that it should be sold.

Problem: Since title is in dad's name, the title company insists on documentation in the property records, for the heirs (the four children) to be able to sign closing documents.

Solution: We file an Affidavit of Heirship with facts regarding the heirs and their respective shares. The children can then present the Affidavit to third parties when dealing with, or selling the house. We would also draft a Consent and Distribution Agreement for the proceeds of sale if needed.

2. ASSUMPTION OF MORTGAGE

Mr. Dee recently died, leaving behind a wife. His name was the only name on the deed to the house. His wife would now like to take over the mortgage payments and have her name added to the deed and all property records.

Problem: The mortgage company is refusing to cooperate and says that the wife will have to pay off the balance on the loan, to be able to keep the house.

Solution: We review the deed to see if the mortgage is assumable. If so, we request an assumption packet, complete and submit it for the wife, and follow up on the file. If not assumable, the wife will need to refinance in her own name.

3. DEBT COLLECTION DEFENSE

Deb was recently served with a citation and petition stating that she has been sued by a creditor. The petition states that Deb owes the credit company the sum of $50,000.

Problem: Deb recognizes the debt and would like to take care of it but does not have $50,000 at this time. She would also like to avoid having a judgment on her credit report.

Solution: We file an answer to the lawsuit and negotiate a settlement (often less than 50%), along with a repayment plan that allows Deb to repay the debt over a period of up to 24 months. We make sure the creditor waives any attorney fees, and that no judgment is taken against Deb. If the creditor insists on a judgment due to the lengthy repayment period, we negotiate for the judgment not to be filed, and ensure that such judgment is fully released following final payment.

4. FORECLOSURE (HOME EQUITY LOAN)

Helen is 3 months behind on her mortgage payments due to a temporary job loss. The lender has filed an Application for Foreclosure, asking the court for an order allowing lender to foreclose. Helen believes that in about 3 months, she will have enough funds to catch up on the past due payments.

Problem: Helen does not want to lose her home and needs more time to come up with the mortgage payments but the lender is refusing to work with her and bent on foreclosure.

Solution: We file a response within the required timeframe (38 days in Texas), then negotiate reinstatement with lender. If left with no option, and there are legal grounds, we sue the lender in a separate lawsuit, which will stop the foreclosure case automatically. The law may be different in other states.

5. FORECLOSURE (REINSTATEMENT)

Harry is 6 months behind on his mortgage payments due to serious health issues. The mortgage lender had previously sent Harry a Notice of Foreclosure Sale. The foreclosure is scheduled for next Tuesday. Harry believes that in about 6 months, he will have enough money to catch up on the past due payments.

Problem: Harry does not want to lose his home but needs a few months to come up with a plan for repayment. The lender is refusing to work with him at this point.

Solution: We will put in a request for detailed accounting on the loan history, and ask that the foreclosure be stopped pending the completion of the accounting process. Afterwards, we will negotiate a loan modification, forbearance or reinstatement. If necessary (and appropriate), we will sue the lender to gain some leverage in negotiations.

6. HEIRSHIP PROCEEDING

Bill and Sue are brother and sister born to the same mother. Their father was never in the picture, and their mother died without a will, leaving behind the two children and her live-in partner. She only owned a house at her death and the partner still lives in the house and claims common law marriage.

Problem: Partner says the mother left him the house but has no paperwork to prove his claim. Their mother's name is the only name on the deed. Bob and Sue claim that their mother always said she would leave her house to her children.

Solution: We file an Heirship Proceeding to determine the true heirs, who are entitled to ownership of the house. The court will decide whether the partner is a legal heir.

7. OWNER FINANCED MORTGAGE

Bess wants to buy property from Sal but cannot qualify for a conventional loan and doesn't have enough cash to buy the property outright. There is no mortgage or lien on the property and Sal holds the title free and clear.

Problem: Bess wants to know how she can buy the property with very little cash down.

Solution: Bess must convince Sal to owner finance the sale and get Sal to agree to hold a note on the property. Once Sal agrees and the parties work out the terms, the lawyer will put together owner finance documents. At minimum, we will draft a promissory note, deed of trust, and a warranty deed with vendor's lien.

8. PARTITION/ FORCED SALE OF REAL ESTATE

Brad and Sally are brother and sister. Their mother died without a will and left her house to both Brad and Sally. There is no debt owed on the property.

Problem: Brad wishes to live in the house since he doesn't currently have a home. Sally is well-to-do and insists on selling the property so she can get her share out of the proceeds of sale. They can't agree on what to do and Brad cannot afford to buy Sally out of her share of the property.

Solution: We file a Partition action on behalf of the sister, in order to force sale of the property. If the property is not easily partitioned as in the case of a multi-unit property, then the court will likely grant an order for sale of the whole property so that Sally can get her share out of the proceeds of sale. Upon sale of the property, Brad will also get his 50% share and may then do whatever he wishes with his share.

9. QUIET TITLE ACTION

Ten years ago, Mr. Sal sold property to Ms. Bee for an agreed price, using a quitclaim deed. Ms. Bee would now like to sell the property to a third party. The title company refuses to issue a title policy and has stated that the quitclaim deed is insufficient for purposes of issuing a title policy. The title company wants to see a warranty deed signed by Mr. Sal or a court order confirming that Ms. Bee has clear title.

Problem: Ms. Bee has no idea where Mr. Sal is because ten years have passed since the original sale. Neither the realtor nor the private investigator has been able to locate Mr. Sal.

Solution: We file a Quiet Title action to obtain a court order from the court, confirming Ms. Bee as the rightful owner of the property. We will have to first properly serve the missing Mr. Sal via notice in a newspaper, and attend a court hearing.

10. WRAP-AROUND MORTGAGE

Beth wants to buy property from Sam but Sam still has a mortgage on the property. The mortgage is not assumable and Beth knows she cannot qualify for a conventional loan yet doesn't have cash to buy the property outright.

Problem: Beth would like to figure out a way to buy the property without needing to get approved by Sam's lender.

Solution: We'll put together wrap mortgage documents to allow Beth to purchase the property subject to the original mortgage. At minimum, we'll draft a wrap promissory note, a wrap deed of trust and a wrap warranty deed. Sam can elect to collect monthly payments from Beth, then pay the original lender monthly. Once the agreed balance is paid off, Beth will own the property and lender's and Sam's lien will be released.

LEGAL SENSE

KNOWLEDGE IS POWER

In this section, I have added updated versions of select posts from my law firm blog. This is in an effort to provide general information and useful tips on legal issues that clients commonly encounter. For more specific information, please contact our law firm directly. You may also view more recent blog posts at www.everymanlaw.com I hope you find this compilation helpful.

U.S. LEGAL SYSTEM – HOW IT WORKS

Here is a quick overview of our legal system: the way it's designed to work, and the way it actually works. Knowing some limitations of our legal system may help minimize stress and frustration when navigating the legal world.

Our legal system is made up of rules that we can group into three main categories:

1. *Rules of Law* – e.g. statutes and codes tell judges how to decide a case
2. *Procedural Rules* – e.g. pre-trial and trial procedures that tell lawyers/ parties how to file papers, conduct a case etc.
3. *Rules of Evidence* e.g. rules on what can and cannot be brought into court to prove a case

The Way the Legal System Is Designed to Work

In theory, all the rules listed above will help guide the judge or jury in figuring out the truth so as to resolve disputes fairly. Each side will have a chance to follow the procedural and evidentiary rules to present evidence that is most favorable to their side. This will supposedly even out the playing field. Also, these laws are not supposed to change too rapidly so that there aren't constant surprises and everyone can reasonably anticipate how the law works.

How the Legal System Works

Since no system is perfect, the legal system doesn't exactly work the way it's set up to work. Here are some reasons why I believe that the system isn't as predictable or reliable as it is in theory:

Some variables that affect legal outcomes:

1. Lawyers and judges don't always follow the rules (hey, they are only human!)
2. The U.S. has an incredibly complex web of rules.
3. The system can be very slow moving.
4. The rules won't always get you a fair result.
5. The truth doesn't always come out.
6. One judge may see things differently from another judge (probably due to personality differences, personal outlook and attitudes, background etc.)

Is it fair that so many variables are at play? I can't say. However, I am here to remind you of these limitations so that you are ready for any outcome when you leave your case up to the court to decide.

Remember also that no two cases are exactly alike. That is a big part of the gamble where litigation is concerned. If feasible and applicable in your case, you can always try to settle out of court Settlement often allows you to structure a closer win-win situation than you would get from a trial. The gavel quite often falls heavily to one side.

If your case does end up going before a judge or jury, the best you and your lawyer can do is to make sure to plan your case properly, prepare thoroughly for trial, and then present your best case to the court. The rest is out of your hands.

COURTROOM ETIQUETTE

Most people are uncomfortable or nervous when in court. I believe that if you follow most of the suggestions below, you will have a smoother ride through the corridors of justice. Keep in mind that these are general tips only. As always, use your best judgment when confronted with a specific situation.

Ten Tips & Tricks, Hints & Hurdles

1. Always try to answer the exact question asked, and answer in a few words! No more, no less.
2. Do show up early to deal with parking, security, locating the right room etc.
3. Do dress formal or semi-formal. Show up well-groomed, with clean, pressed clothing. Nothing too tight or flashy, nothing too revealing or low-cut.
4. Do speak courteously to clerks and all other parties involved in your case.
5. Do address the judge as "Your Honor" or "Judge."
6. Do say "Yes" instead of Yeah, Yep, Yup or any other variation of that word.
7. Do leave anger management issues at home.
8. Don't roll your eyes, snicker or mumble under your breath.
9. Don't talk out of turn, or over anyone else. This includes the judge who is going to decide your case!
10. Even when the other party or the judge is lying or seriously pissing you off, do maintain your composure!

Bonus Tip: Dress comfortably, but appropriately. Be respectful and polite. Relax. Remember, an overly aggressive attitude only gets results in TV courtrooms.

BRACING YOURSELF FOR LITIGATION

Many of us enjoy the shenanigans of TV character Saul Goodman (S'all Good Man). He is infamous for encouraging litigation with wisdom such as *"Who can you sue?; Sue 'Em Now!"* The truth is that litigation is more stressful than pleasurable. Perhaps one of the parties has heeded Saul's advice, or perhaps litigation is unavoidable. How do you brace yourself for what's coming?

Here are four ways to prepare for the mental, emotional and financial demands of a lawsuit:

1. *Budget Money*: Get a rough estimate for attorney fees and court costs then double it. Lawyers can't always anticipate the level of resistance, rigidity, or hostility that you or the other party will put up. The more resistance, rigidity and hostility, the higher the costs.
2. *Budget Time:* Schedule time off well in advance for consultations, court hearings, mediation, depositions, etc. Remember to engage the help of babysitters, co-workers, and bosses ahead of time.
3. *Gather Information:* Ask your lawyer for a checklist of needed documents. Start early. You may need to complete questionnaires, help gather documents from banks, vendors, insurers, fund managers etc.
4. *Plan R & R:* You can expect higher than normal stress levels and periods of heightened anxiety. Rest, relaxation and hobbies will help. A visit with a therapist is not a bad idea either, especially in the case of family law litigation.

Finally, do a cost-benefit analysis for tasks that you'll handle yourself rather than delegate to a lawyer, and figure out the opportunity cost (potential loss of not outsourcing the task.)

KEEP CALM & LET THE ATTORNEY HANDLE IT

Easier said than done right? Well, you can at least keep sane and let the attorney handle it. You've somehow found yourself in court (maybe you sued someone, or someone sued you). Either way, it's seldom a pleasant experience.

You can still stay sane while doing all you can to help your case. If you've hired an attorney, then take advantage of being able to outsource your worries. A good attorney will provide some reassurance or at least let you know the things that are actually within your control. No use worrying about the things outside of your control right?

To keep sane during your case, here are some Dos:

1. DO check your facts and write up a timeline or account of events complete with names, dates, etc.
2. DO gather and organize helpful documents and correspondence.
3. DO set clear goals for your desired outcome and prioritize those goals.
4. DO make a clear plan of action but remain flexible and open to alternative plans.

KEEP CALM & STAY SANE DURING LITIGATION

Let's examine some Don'ts for keeping cool, calm and collected during a legal battle. These are true whether you have a lawyer or not. If you have a lawyer, your primary objective is to get out of the lawyer's way! It is to your advantage that your lawyer isn't hindered in any way and is able to effectively advocate your position.

To keep sane during your case, here are some Don'ts:

1. DON'T withhold hard facts from your lawyer. The truth usually comes out and at the most inconvenient of times. Avoidable surprises are a no-no and tend to hurt your case.
2. DON'T make your ultimate goal a continuously moving target. You will come across scattered and tentative both to the court and to the opposing side.
3. DON'T share details of your case strategy with the opposing side (including via friends or social media). Refer any case related questions to your attorney.
4. DON'T make promises or offers relating to your case without first consulting or informing your attorney. Your lawyer is there to help check any blind spots.
5. DON'T micromanage your lawyer. If you don't have faith in the lawyer you hired, find another one pronto!

These tips should help reduce the stress and anxiety that comes with litigation. You will also be proactive by doing your part to avoid hurting your case. Remember, anything you say or do is often used against you in the court of law.

GOING PRO SE (REPRESENTING YOURSELF)

My advice is that you try to get a lawyer if there is more than $5000 at stake, or if child custody or real property is at stake. At the very least, you should consult a lawyer first. A lot of lawyers waive the initial consultation fee or offer a reduced rate for the initial consultation. Some lawyers will even provide limited scope representation such as reviewing court drafts/documents and providing guidance for procedural rules without your having to put down a hefty retainer.

So, you have reviewed all of the above and have decided that you will rather represent yourself. Here are some cool tips to help you in court:

Court Prep - Think in terms of twos:

1. **Two Issues/ Defenses**: list the two main issues that bring you to court, or two main defenses (if you are the defendant.)
2. **Two Supporting Documents**: locate the two most important documents you can use to support your facts and arguments – contracts, receipts, bills, exhibits, affidavits, photos, letters, emails etc.
3. **Two Requests**: list two things you want the court or judge to do. *Example*: Dismiss the case and order you to pay nothing; Rule in your favor and grant you a certain amount in judgment; Rule in your favor and order the opposing party to return your property etc.

Put this 2 x 2 x 2 together before your hearing. The more organized and clear you are, the better your chances in court.

Questions to Ask in Preparation for Court Hearing:

- What court is the hearing in?
- What date/time is the hearing?
- What is the hearing about?
- What are the rules for getting my evidence in front of the judge/court?
- Do I need to bring extra copies of my exhibits?
- Are there any pretrial issues or deadlines that I need to know about?
- Are there any notice rules that I need to know about?
- Are there any court forms that I can use?

RISKY BUSINESS – CO-SIGNING A LOAN

Just say NO. If you can avoid it, don't! If you must, then you deserve to be fully versed on all the risks. This is one where there is barely any advantage and a lot of potentially negative exposure.

PROs

1. Can potentially help build your credit if payments are made on time.
2. Your credit profile will likely improve if the debt is successfully paid off.

CONs

1. If the primary borrower dies, you are still on the hook for the balance owed.
2. In case of a default, you are each 100% responsible for repayment.
3. Late payments by primary borrower will hurt your credit.
4. Non-payment by primary borrower may expose you to lawsuits/ foreclosure.
5. Your debt-to-income ratio may affect your ability to obtain new credit.
6. You may be unable to qualify for a second mortgage or a home loan.

To sum it up, if you must co-sign, make sure it is for an amount you can afford to pay off or afford to lose. Know the terms of the loan (especially the duration), and instruct the lender to notify you of any late payments.

QUICK CHECKLIST FOR ANY CONTRACT

Have you ever entered into a contract to later feel duped? If you signed of your own free will, it will be difficult to claim duress. Most courts will not find coercion simply because you now regret the deal or believe the other party "pushed" you into a bargain that wasn't in your best interest. Duress typically includes the use of threats and/or harassment.

The checklist below will should help avoid those situations, and help whenever you have the opportunity to draft or make modifications to a contract.

Checklist for Your Contract

1. **Who? What? When? Where?** This one is self-explanatory.
2. **Is time of the essence**? If so, specify the expected delivery date(s).
3. **Is particular quality or materials required**? Provide specifications.
4. **What are the due dates for payments?** Specify amounts and due dates.
5. **What's the break-even point**? How will you know when you've turned a profit or bargain (if applicable)?
6. **Plan for unknowns?** What happens in case of delays, hidden costs, third parties, change requests etc.
7. **What are minimum acceptable terms?** Time, money, quantity, quality etc.
8. **Is the final agreement in writing?** Is the writing clear, detailed, and signed by all parties?

If you keep a checklist like this one, you can enter into simple contracts knowing that you've done your due diligence. For complex contracts, consult a lawyer. If a deal doesn't feel right, WALK, or stick to your lowest acceptable terms!

LOVED ONES & WRITTEN AGREEMENTS

Written agreements vary from the very informal such as an "I owe You" to the very formal and can save you a lot of headache and heartache. Whatever the form, any writing evidencing the agreement is better than no writing at all. Especially in situations where real property or a large sum of money is involved, or where time is of the essence, the agreement should be in writing.

You already know the wisdom of not loaning to family and friends, what you cannot afford to give away. However, sometimes it is unavoidable to enter into agreements with family and friends. In that case, it is best to get the agreement in writing. When it comes to family, friends, and loved ones, contracts tend to be verbal and informal. Sometimes, the terms of these verbal agreements are clearly thought out and clearly communicated, but often times, they are not.

Do you feel a little weird or uncomfortable asking a loved one to sign a written agreement? Or even reading this? No worries. On the next page, I'll show you how to present it such that it is not terribly awkward for you or them.

4 Reasons to Get Your Agreement in Writing

1. **It memorializes the important terms of the agreement.** At minimum, any contract requires the following terms: *What? When? How Much? By Whom?*
2. **Memories fade, and worse, even change with time**. The terms of a verbal agreement are far more open to interpretation. To ensure that all parties know what is to be performed by both sides, get it in writing so you don't ever have to have a he-said, she-said verbal gymnastics down the road.

3. **People tend to keep promises made in writing, signed by them**, more than an abstract verbal promise. Help your friend, family or loved one save face by reminding them of their written promise so that they are held accountable and have a chance to rise up to the occasion.
4. **Protects you and your relationships**. It is better to have a writing to avoid future disagreements, than to lose a friend or loved one over the inevitable confusion, miscommunication, or resentment that will arise from conflicts over verbal agreements. It also protects you if you ever end up needing to have a lawyer or court enforce your agreement.

How to Propose a Written Agreement to Loved Ones

Use any of the following suggested phrases, or a variation, as needed:

- "We better write this down so that there is no confusion in the future."
- "May I suggest that we put this in writing so that we are both on the same page as to what we've agreed to?"
- "We should put this down in writing so as to avoid any miscommunication and to have something to refer to, as I cannot rely on my memory."

Finally, offer to be the scribe. If needed, get a lawyer to help – trust me, the upfront cost is nothing compared to what I've seen people lose when they omit to get a written agreement. Take it upon yourself to get the terms down on paper, and make sure that each person dates and signs the document. Imagine how much messier a dispute can get when there isn't any writing at all to clarify things or refresh memories.

THE EMPOWERED CLIENT

For effective representation to take place, the attorney needs the client and the client needs the attorney. I have yet to come across a case where I didn't depend on the client for one or more of the following: the client's account of events; relevant documents in the client's possession; client's signature on court and other documents; or the client's appearance in court /mediation/ deposition etc.

However, given the context of an attorney-client relationship, the client often stands to gain or lose the most in terms of the outcome of the legal matter. Yet, for various reasons some clients are better than others at participating in their own case and working collaboratively with their attorney.

Considering what's at stake, wouldn't you as a client want to know if there was a way to positively affect the outcome of your case? This is what I call "The Empowered Client." The Empowered Client knows that he/she can influence the outcome of the case, but also knows that he/she can affect the enthusiasm of the attorney.

For a successful team approach, the following must be understood and acknowledged by both attorney and client:

1. The attorney and client are united with the sole purpose of resolving a legal issue.
2. The legal issue is the equivalent of a project.
3. The attorney is a project manager and manages the client's expectations, the project and the project team.
4. The attorney and client are equally responsible for the outcome of the project.
5. The client has the choice to support or be an ally to the attorney, or become an obstacle.

6. Supporters or allies provide whatever is needed for the project to succeed.
7. Obstacles delay, derail, antagonize the project team, and generally sabotage the project.
8. Projects where the client is an obstacle will always be more extensive and more expensive.

For the best possible outcome, the client must choose the project manager (attorney) wisely, then get out of the way and be an ally or supporter of the project team.

A lot more can be said on ways in which the attorney and the empowered client can support each other in positively influencing the outcome of the legal matter. My hope is that the list above helps get the conversation started with yourself, or your attorney.

MAKING THE MOST OF YOUR CONSULT

We all go into discussions and meetings with some sort of agenda in mind, to varying degrees of detail depending on our personal tendencies. Clients that come to a meeting with a clear agenda almost always get more out of that meeting. Below are some ways to make the agenda work for you such that you can intentionally get the most out of any discussion. I believe in keeping things simple so I will use the **rule of three** in illustrating.

1. ***Bring 3 things to the table***. Go into the discussion with 3 specific things in each of the following categories, that you will convey to the attorney/ firm:

(i) 3 Qualities or expertise that drew you to the firm.
(ii) 3 Questions, issues or needs that you want help with.
(iii) 3 Qualities of yours e.g. cooperativeness, willingness or ability to listen, research, take suggestions, do leg work etc.

2. ***Take Away 3 things***. Leave the discussion with 3 things that you have just learned from the meeting. Each item must clearly address the following:

(i) What question does this answer for me?
(ii) What need does this meet?
(iii) How do I implement this knowledge?

3. ***Leave with 3 action items***. Do not leave the meeting until you clearly have 3 items for you to take action on. Each item should fit into one or more of the following categories:

(i) Needs immediate action.
(ii) Needs some more research.
(iii) Needs action at a specified time/date in the future.

INITIAL CLIENT INTERVIEW I

WHAT TO EXPECT

Not quite sure what to expect at the initial consultation or interview? No sweat! This will give you a good overview. Some law firms have an initial consultation handled by a non-attorney, then have a follow-up client interview. Other firms just have the one initial meeting with an attorney. While different firms conduct the initial client interview differently, there are certain things you can expect at any interview.

The Initial Interview

I'll first like to point out that this is an informal meeting and you don't need to worry about dressing formal or rehearsing your story. Usually, this is your first chance to put a face to the attorney/firm and vice versa. Often, it is also your first chance to tell your story to an attorney. The attorney will then be able to decide four main things (at the meeting or after a couple of days of review):

1. Is there a valid legal case?
2. Is there a good chance of prevailing?
3. What are some feasible options for this case?
4. Do we want to represent this particular individual?

Before the Meeting

You've been sued, are thinking of suing someone, or just want to protect yourself legally. You set an appointment to see the attorney. The attorney and or his/her staff will pre-screen you by asking you some generic questions. This is to start developing an idea of all the qualifiers listed above. You may receive an Initial Interview form to fill out and bring to the meeting, or asked to fill one out at the meeting. This form goes over your basic information such as Name, Address, Reason for Your Visit, How You Will Pay for Services etc. Once all of this preliminary stuff is out of the way, your interview is next. The initial interview can take anywhere between 45 minutes to an hour, and sometimes longer.

How the Meeting Plays Out

Most attorneys or intake staff start with an open-ended question. Example: Tell me what's going on…" Most will also allow you to freely tell your story uninterrupted the first time. This is because frequent interruptions may cause you to lose your train of thought or become stressed out. Let's be honest, you probably already feel slightly uncomfortable sitting across from a lawyer, contemplating legal action.

It may be helpful to tell your story in chronological order of time or events, but feel free to tell your story however you want. Don't worry, the attorney and intake staff are trained to get the most important parts of your story. Some will take notes as you are talking. Once you stop talking, they will ask you questions for clarification and to help fill in any gaps.

You may then be told how much the legal services will cost. Attorney fees can be an hourly rate, a flat fee, contingency fee, or a combination. You may be informed that out-of-pocket expenses are billed in addition to attorney fees. Some law firms will give you an estimate of related expenses such as court filing fees. You may also be informed that all the quotes are only an estimate. If there is a retainer required, you will be informed. Retainer is a term used loosely and is most often simply a down-payment for the services to be rendered. True retainers are seldom used these days.

Caveat

Keep in mind that what you think is super important may not be the thing the attorney focuses on. Don't let this discourage you. It is likely because the attorney's task is to gather the legally relevant parts of the story. The fact that an issue seems to be a big deal to you, seems morally or ethically wrong, or seems obviously unfair, doesn't mean that the particular event or occurrence is legally relevant to your case. However, the attorney should still make note of such concerns.

Closing

<u>One of 4 things will happen:</u>

1. The attorney declines representation (this doesn't necessarily mean you don't have a valid case);
2. You decide not to use the services of the attorney;
3. You and the attorney mutually agree to the terms of representation (an agreement will be signed and payment secured or arranged); <u>OR</u>
4. The attorney needs a couple of days to make a decision on whether to represent you.

INITIAL CLIENT INTERVIEW II

IS THERE A GOOD FIT?

Let's discuss how the attorney/ firm may come to the conclusion of whether or not to take your case. Attorneys consider many factors so I will only cover those factors that I think are within your control.

What the Attorney Is Thinking While You're Talking

First and foremost, the attorney is hopefully listening attentively to your words. In an attempt to figure out whether the music matches your words, he or she is also listening to what you aren't saying. Attorneys have to be detectives too. They read you while you are in front of them and watch to see if your personality type spells trouble. **Mainly, the attorney wants to know the following things**:

- Are you fair-minded?
- Are you somewhat truthful?
- Are you high-maintenance?

Fair-Minded. The truth is that there are always two or more sides to any story. So, it is a given that you will tell your story from your own perspective (as you should!) This is not a problem. What raises red flags is a complete lack of willingness or complete inability to see things from any other perspective, or to take any kind of responsibility in the events that occurred.

Somewhat Truthful. Allow me to explain. We will all tell *OUR* story from our own skewed point of view. This is why I think appearing *somewhat truthful* is satisfactory under the circumstances. Attorneys really don't expect truthfulness of saint-like proportions from you. However, outright lies won't help your case either – whether in front of the lawyer or in court. So, when telling your story, be as honest as much as you can, meaning stick to hard facts and try not to exaggerate or embellish.

High-Maintenance. This one is my favorite. You have potential clients that come across as difficult, demanding, bossy. arrogant, entitled, or as bullies. They already *know* how to win the case, already have the strategy laid out, and just need an attorney (puppet) to carry out their clever, fail-proof plan. It is little wonder that any good lawyer would steer clear of these types. Most lawyers would likely decline to represent such individuals.

Here are some indicators that make you appear high-maintenance to an attorney:

- This isn't your first, second or third rodeo
- You sued your previous attorney(s)
- You decided not to pay your previous attorney(s)
- This is your n^{th} client interview on this matter
- You *know* this is a slam-dunk case
- You call and email the firm/attorney constantly
- You are overly emotional
- You come across as overly cold
- You come across as overly vindictive
- You have a tendency to come across as a jerk

The next page covers things that you as the client, can look out for at the interview to make sure that you select the best attorney for your situation.

INITIAL CLIENT INTERVIEW III

SCREEN THE ATTORNEY

You are the client and in that sense, the employer. Though often called the Initial Consultation or Client Interview, YOU are also interviewing the lawyer for the job! Okay, so what do you do when you want to hire someone? Those same common-sense things apply in this situation. Don't be intimidated just because the roles are a bit reversed i.e. you the employer are actually traveling to see the person to be employed, on their home turf.

Word of Caution: Don't go in with the attitude that the attorney is a puppet to be controlled. They are there to guide you and collaborate with you, not take commands per se.

Some important things to ask the attorney that you are thinking of employing:

1. What is your experience or background in this type of matter?
2. Do you honestly think this is worth pursuing?
3. What is your success rate in these types of cases?
4. Have you ever been sued by a client?
5. Have you ever had any disciplinary action against you as a lawyer?
6. Can you estimate how long it will take to conclude this case?
7. Can you estimate how much this will cost me out-of-pocket?
8. What is your policy on communicating the progress of the case to the client?

These are just a few questions but should get the dialogue going. Although some of the questions may not get you direct answers, you can learn as much from the way the attorney answers or doesn't answer a question.

Don't forget soft-skills and bedside manners issues such as the attorney's personality or what vibe you are getting from him/her. This matters because you want to work with someone that doesn't rub you the wrong way.

You also want to watch out for the lawyer's ability to listen, understand, etc. Pay close attention to any hint of arrogance, condescension, irritation or indifference. These may all lead to personality clashes in the future.

The bottom-line is that even a very competent lawyer can be unlikeable and unpopular. You shouldn't have to risk losing your case purely based on your lawyer's reputation. That may seem far-fetched and unfair, but it happens. For that reason, we are all better off picking a lawyer who has a good reputation with peers and the judges/ courts.

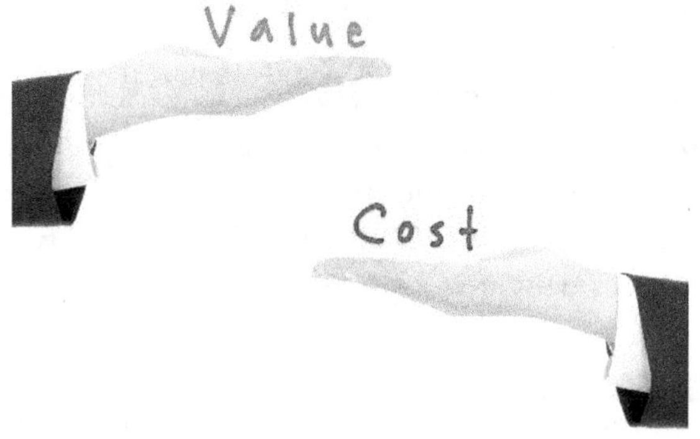

WHAT'S YOUR CASE WORTH TO YOU?

What is a glass of water worth? $1? $100? It depends on whether I'm in the desert or in the city. Most lawyers aren't able to quote an absolute price since not all pieces are within the lawyer's control. There are variables that are difficult to predict, such as unknown facts, the client's attitude, opposing party /counsel's attitudes, judges, jury etc.

It's unrealistic for firms to break down their pricing model for you, which is why I have attempted to explain the value-based pricing of services. This will help you better gauge the true cost of a service rather than simply focusing on the dollar figure or time factor. There is a lot more that goes into delivery of services, especially if you want quality representation and hourly billing isn't always available nor does it always make sense for every case.

Some criteria used for pricing services:

1. ***Value added*** (benefit gained or negative consequence avoided)
2. ***Labor*** (time and effort devoted)
3. Materials (documents produced, expert reports, court transcripts etc.)
4. ***Difficulty / Complexity*** (special expertise required.)
5. ***Speed of Delivery*** (time constraint imposed by client, court, or other parties)
6. ***Ultimate Result/Outcome*** (finesse, quality of services delivered.)

Next time you're quoted a price or quoted attorney fees, weigh what each item above is worth to your particular case. You can then make your choice with full confidence that you're making the best-informed decision for you.

NEGOTIATING LIKE A PRO

Every single day, we are negotiating something. So, let's explore how we can further develop this natural instinct. When professional athletes train before any feat or competition, they train with the end in mind. They almost always visualize themselves succeeding at whatever they set out to accomplish. The truth is, even the best of the best can't just roll out of bed and compete without preconditioning for weeks or months well in advance of the big day.

If we don't keep our negotiation muscles well-conditioned, they may let us down at crucial points. So, how do we go about doing this conditioning thing that I mention? Well, I am going to suggest the following things that I have observed generally tend to work. In short, these are some tried and true techniques – use with caution or you will be overwhelmed by the ease with which you are able to get others to adopt your point of view or your vision.

1. ***Seek first to understand, then to be Understood***.

This one is straight from the book 7 Habits of Highly Effective People by Stephen Covey.) This is self-explanatory but I will add that you can practice this with your friends, family, significant other etc. It is actually harder than it sounds. Seeking to understand is not the same as faking active listening. Make sure you understand and can clearly articulate the speaker's position at the end of listening to him/her.

2. ***Get clear on the following things before you attempt to communicate your position:***

a) Your Motive
b) Your Intention(s)
c) Your Ideal Desired Outcome
d) Your Level of Attachment to Such Outcome
e) Alternative Acceptable Outcomes
f) Unacceptable Outcomes
g) What Relationship you want to have with the other party after your communications

3. ***Based on your understanding of the other party's position, answer the following questions:***

1. Are they firm in their position? (how firm?)
2. What is their underlying motive? (try to pin it down to one or two max)
3. In what way is my desired outcome (or other acceptable outcome) compatible with their underlying motive?

The reality is that there are only so many motives that drive our rigid adherence to a position – top four being fear, uncertainty, distrust, and self-preservation. When examined closely, we will find that all these are really just different manifestations of the same thing - FEAR.

The other common motives are economic gain (money, time, productivity), and feeding the ego. These I lump together under self-preservation – again, a derivative of FEAR.

4. ***Start communicating your position with emphasis on how your position is similar to the other party's underlying needs/concerns.***

If you can help it, refrain from using the word *motive* outwardly as it sometimes carries a negative connotation. Stay calm and repeat your understanding of the fact that even though your positions appear incompatible on the surface, they are quite similar when you look closer into the things driving those positions. No matter how obviously different your goals are, you should be able to say this with a straight face and, hopefully you both will start believing it soon enough.

Once you find a commonality and point that out to the other party, this serves to form a baseline to work from, and an unlikely alliance develops. Distrust is a bit lessened and guards aren't up as much. The combination of hearing them out first, and then pointing out the similarities between you, can be useful in getting people's guards down.

5. ***Now it's time to pitch your position***. Well, try not to pitch but rather, tie it into the similarities you already outlined above, with emphasis on how it could be an acceptable outcome for both parties.

Hopefully, this practice yields results for you. An added bonus is the ability to leave the negotiation table without burning the table (burning bridges, burning tables.) It really is much easier to get people to come around when they believe the final decision was at least partly their idea.

WHAT'S ON YOUR CREDIT REPORT?

Do you know what's on your credit reports? Are you looking to make your credit score even better? Talk to a professional that can analyze your credit reports and guide you in what actions to take to start improving your score. Most credit reports have errors in them that can be fixed to boost a credit score.

As of 2015, according to FICO, the national average credit score in the U.S. is 630. Credit scores can go as high as 900 and a score of 750+ is ideal. ***The credit score affects all aspects of life such as interest rates, credit limit, renting, insurance quotes, employment etc.***

I recently met with a top executive at Regions Bank. Their secured credit line program got my attention as very few banks offer this program and those banks that do offer it tend to require a hefty initial deposit. At Regions Bank (as of 2016), this type of account can be opened for under $300! This is an excellent way to rehab one's credit rating because Regions Bank reports monthly to the credit bureaus which has the result of quickly improving the credit score.

Contact your local branch if you have questions about the secured credit line program. For readers that prefer to speak directly to the executive that I mentioned above, you may email to william.ownbey@regions.com.

Neither I nor my firm has any affiliation with Regions Bank. If your current bank offers a similar program, it should be just as beneficial as the one offered by Regions Bank. Be sure to do your due diligence before enrolling in any program.

GARNISHMENTS & OLD JUDGMENTS

Old judgments resurfacing out of the blue can be quite disruptive. Perhaps the person didn't know about the case at all, failed to follow up on the case, or didn't receive notice of the final judgment. Either way, it's a very nasty surprise when an employer or bank forwards you a Notice of Garnishment.

Judgments can lie dormant for years and years and accrue interest all that time. In Texas, judgment creditors may renew the judgment every 10 years. Imagine having to cough up $20,000 for a $5,000 judgment! So, my suggestion is that you make sure the judgment stays dead, not just dormant. ***Here are some proactive things you can do:***

1. Open all correspondence.
2. Show up to all hearings.
3. Obtain the final disposition from the court.
4. Appeal within the time allowed under the law.
5. Settle the judgment (reduction is often possible).
6. Determine whether bankruptcy makes sense.

Watch out for Out-of-State cases:

Out-of-state judgment creditors sometimes wrongfully submit a garnishment request to employers or banks. They <u>cannot legally</u> do this without first registering the judgment in a Texas court (domesticating the judgment). This process is designed to give the debtor notification of the old judgment, and a chance to handle the issue. However, Judgment creditors <u>can</u> and <u>do</u> get away with not domesticating the judgment because their actions aren't challenged correctly (or at all). If you receive a Notice of Garnishment from your bank or employer, contact a lawyer asap! You will need professional help to put a stop to it.

HOA FORECLOSURES AND YOUR RIGHTS

If you ever receive collection notices or foreclosure notices from your Homeowners' Association, don't panic! The issue can be easily handled by knowing your rights.

Myth: HOAs can't foreclose and get a property worth hundreds of thousands of dollars, for a mere failure to pay association dues.

Fact: It's quite absurd, but it is true that the HOA *can* in fact foreclose, and take ownership, regardless of the market value and regardless of whether you owe $500 or $5000!

Changes in the Law: A new law went into effect in 2012 that requires HOAs to work with homeowners to get any delinquency resolved, and requires the HOAs to seek a foreclosure through the court. Prior to 2012, HOAs used to be able to bypass the court system by doing a non-judicial foreclosure.

New Protections under 2012 HOA Laws

- HOAs must work with delinquent homeowners to come up with a payment plan that is no shorter than 3 months.
- Collection fees may not be tacked on until a 30-day notice to cure (resolve) has first been provided.
- HOAs must obtain a court order to be able to foreclose.
- Debt must be more than 60 days old before any foreclosure proceeding is started.
- MOST IMPORTANTLY: Homeowners can vote to remove the "power to foreclose" provision from their HOA's rules. 67% vote is all that is needed.

OWNER FINANCE VS. ASSUMPTION VS. WRAP

Due to the complex structure of these real estate deals, we highly recommend that you get a lawyer to draft or review the contract documents prior to signing anything. ***As the saying goes, pay now, or pay much more later.*** Here are notable distinctions for these forms of non-conventional financing:

Owner Finance

Seller has title free and clear and is willing to hold a note for a period of time. Usually, there is a fixed number of years when installment payments are being made by Buyer. At the end of that period, a balloon payment is due. If Buyer is unable to make the balloon payment, the whole sale is forfeited and Seller may retain title as if Buyer had simply been renting.

Assumption

Buyer steps in to assume the loan that Seller has with the mortgage lender. Most mortgages created after 2005 are non-assumable. The few that are assumable often require a familial relationship between Buyer and Seller. Buyer often has to qualify for the loan independently although the screening process isn't as stringent as it is for a conventional mortgage.

Wrap Around Mortgage (Wrap)

Seller has a mortgage loan and Buyer buys from Seller subject to that existing mortgage (without assuming it). Seller holds a promissory note from Buyer, which normally matures around the same time as the underlying mortgage. Usually, Seller gets monthly payments from Buyer and turns around and makes payment to the mortgage lender. Hence, the term "wrap" i.e. the seller's note from buyer, wraps around the original note.

SERVICER VS. MORTGAGE LENDER

There is often confusion as to the difference between a servicer and a mortgage lender. A quick overview on how to identify the party you're dealing with is to find out which party *owns* the loan account, not merely collecting payments on the account.

The mortgage lender has rights to the underlying mortgage loan (the Note) and the servicer has *only* the right to collect periodic payments (monthly mortgage payments.) The mortgage lender is either the original creditor that advanced a loan to the borrower, or a creditor who purchased the Note from a predecessor lender, or from the original lender.

A servicer on the other hand, is assigned only the right to accept payments on behalf of the lender (including any investors in the case of mortgage-backed securities). Oftentimes, there will be a lender who owns the Note, and a servicer who sends out the mortgage statements, collects payments etc. The lender is required to notify the borrower in writing anytime the servicing of the loan changes. A lender can also service its own loan in which case the lender and servicer are one and the same. During the life of a single mortgage loan, there may be several lenders and servicers.

For this reason, borrowers should always stay vigilant and do the following:

1. Keep good records of all payments.
2. Save copies of all correspondence sent to any lender or servicer.
3. Make sure you receive the lender's notice of new servicer from the lender itself, before sending your payments to any new company.

CASH-FOR-KEYS (POST-FORECLOSURE)

You may have heard of the term cash-for-keys. This is when mortgage lenders pay homeowners to move out after the lender has foreclosed on the mortgage loan. Banks and other mortgage companies will often offer cash-for-keys as an incentive so as to avoid the hassle of eviction court.

Homeowners will sometimes make the best of a bad situation and accept the cash to help towards their relocation costs. Most of the lenders' agents start the offer very low at around $2,000. The most important thing to know is that a lot of the agents have authority to offer up to $10,000. Also, a borrower doesn't have to accept the offer, or even move out, if the borrower truly has legitimate grounds for contesting the foreclosure.

So, depending on the circumstances surrounding a foreclosure, a borrower should try to negotiate a higher cash offer if already inclined to accept the cash-for-keys. If not inclined to accept any cash offer, and also not inclined to move out, the lender will have to sue for eviction. Each party will then have their day in court where they can present their arguments.

The other alternative is to sue the lender for wrongful foreclosure if the foreclosure was wrongfully done. This will almost always keep the borrower in the home for months, or until the wrongful foreclosure lawsuit and underlying title issues are resolved.

Whatever the case, keep in mind that accepting the cash offer and then refusing to move out will jeopardize any wrongful foreclosure claims. So, it is best not to accept any Cash-for-Keys offer if you intend to fight the foreclosure.

This concludes the first edition of *Handle Legal Issues Like a Pro*. Thanks for reading! I look forward to improving and updating the content in the future.

Disclaimer

Nothing in this publication should be construed as specific legal advice for your particular situation. For case-specific legal advice, please contact our office directly. Please note also that most of the content of this book is geared towards Texas state law.

The author has strived to be as accurate and complete as possible in the creation of this book. In practical advice books, like anything else in life, there are no guarantees.

Readers are cautioned to apply their own judgment about their individual circumstances and act accordingly. Readers are advised to seek services of competent professionals in the legal, business, and finance fields as needed.

Author Bio:

Sade is an avid traveler, music lover, foodie, and a self-improvement and empowerment enthusiast.

She is licensed to practice law in the state of Texas and is admitted to the United States Bankruptcy Court. She holds a Texas Mediator license and approaches the practice of law with an attitude of excellence, fairness, and compassion.

She enjoys volunteer work involving children and women, helping on advisory boards, and giving educational presentations to the public on relevant legal issues.

Free Legal Tips, Blog Posts & Video Help:

The author provides free legal tips to friends, clients and potential clients, through the law firm website and Facebook page. These free resources may be accessed by visiting the law firm website on www.everymanlaw.com.

Final Words:

I have found that the more questions I answer for others, the more questions I answer for myself; the more problems I solve for others, the more problems are solved for me.

Till next time,
Dream, Desire, Dare

Sade

www.ingramcontent.com/pod-product-compliance
Lightning Source LLC
Chambersburg PA
CBHW060411190526
45169CB00002B/852

* 9 7 8 1 5 3 3 5 9 5 7 0 6 *